COOL CAREERS
WITHOUT COLLEGE
FOR PEOPLE WHO LOVE
SPORTS

CARLA MOONEY

ROSEN
PUBLISHING®

New York

Published in 2017 by The Rosen Publishing Group, Inc.
29 East 21st Street, New York, NY 10010

First Edition

Library of Congress Cataloging-in-Publication Data

Names: Mooney, Carla, 1970– author.
Title: Cool careers without college for people who love sports / Carla Mooney.
Description: New York : Rosen Publishing, 2017. | Series: Cool careers
  without college | Includes bibliographical references and index.
Identifiers: LCCN 2016022147 | ISBN 9781508172864 (library bound)
Subjects: LCSH: Sports—Vocational guidance—Juvenile literature.
Classification: LCC GV734.3 .M66 2017 | DDC 796.023—dc23
LC record available at https://lccn.loc.gov/2016022147

Manufactured in Malaysia

CONTENTS

INTRODUCTION

Have you ever thought about sports as a career? If so, then read on. The following information is all about careers in sports. Athletes are not the only people who have jobs in sports. It takes all types of people to put together a sporting event and have it aired live on television and on the radio. Read on to learn about some sports career options. You might find that you want to jump into a career in the sports industry. None of the jobs that you will find listed here require a college degree, but they demand what most jobs do: dedication and patience to see results. You do not even need to play sports for the majority of these jobs!

In these chapters, you will read about ten different careers that are

Many people work together to put on a baseball game. In addition to the athletes, coaches, and umpires that appear on television, many people perform jobs behind the scenes to make the game possible.

associated with sports in various ways. Each entry describes a job, the training you may need, and gives resources for more information. Many of the jobs discussed can be merged with another job or worked as a second job while you gain experience. You may never even have thought about some of these jobs. Go ahead and read on to find out all about them. You might discover several interesting career options that you had not thought of before.

CHAPTER 1

SPORTS PHOTOGRAPHER OR VIDEOGRAPHER

According to one well-known saying, a picture is worth a thousand words. Some of the most memorable moments in sports have been captured by a photograph or video. From New York Giant David Tyree's miraculous helmet catch in Super Bowl XLII to boxing champion Muhammad Ali's lighting of the Olympic flame in Atlanta, photographs and videos have documented iconic sports moments. Each image was captured by a talented sports photographer or videographer behind the lens.

A sports photographer or videographer takes pictures or video of sporting events, people, and places. They capture action shots for print, broadcast, and online media sources. They cover sporting events such as football, baseball, basketball, or hockey games. They take pictures and video at track and field events, swim meets, skiing races, and golf tournaments. Some follow individual athletes as they rock climb or surf.

A DAY IN THE LIFE

Sports photographers and videographers use technical expertise and creativity to create images that record an event or tell a story. In a typical day, they might:

- Plan the composition of photographs or video
- Use different photo or video techniques and lighting equipment
- Capture athletes or events in commercial-quality photographs or video
- Use natural or artificial light to enhance the subject
- Transfer images or video from portable memory devices to a computer
- Use editing software to crop, modify, and enhance images and video
- Maintain a digital portfolio of work

Today, most photographers and videographers use digital cameras instead of traditional film cameras. Digital cameras capture images electronically and store them on portable memory devices, like memory cards or flash drives. The digital images can be edited on a computer, using special editing software. During editing, photographers crop or modify photos. They enhance and correct color and add special effects. Some photographers use high-quality printers to produce their own prints.

Boxing legend Muhammad Ali holds the Olympic torch during a 2001 ceremony at Atlanta's Centennial Olympic Park. The torch embarked on a 46-state tour to the 2002 Winter Olympics in Salt Lake City, Utah.

Working conditions in this field vary significantly. While some photographers shoot athletes only, others shoot photos and video at sporting events, which often means working unpredictable hours and being on their feet for long periods of time. Some photographers and videographers capture extreme sports like rock climbing or snowboarding, which may require travel to distant locations.

Some photographers and videographers work full-time for a newspaper, magazine, television station, or website. Photographers and videographers working for publications that provide general sports coverage like ESPN or *Sports Illustrated* will be asked to cover a variety of sports. Photographers and videographers with expertise in an individual sport may work for sport-specific publications like *USA Hockey*, NFL Network, or *Tennis* magazine.

Many sports photographers and videographers work as freelancers, taking on assignments from a variety of clients. In order to get assignments, freelance sports photographers network and develop good relationships with publishers, sports teams, and other groups that hire sports

At a golf tournament, a camera crew films a golfer hitting a shot as the gallery of fans watches. The camera crew is prepared to spend long hours at the course until the tournament's end.

ADVENTURE PHOTOGRAPHER CHRIS NOBLE

Photographer Chris Noble has combined his love of photography and adventure sports into a career. Noble takes photographs of athletes competing against nature, like kayakers, climbers, skiers, and more. Depending on the subject, Noble works on land or water, in wild places around the world. He has shot photos in many remote locations, including Denali, Everest, the mountains of the Alps, and the jungles of Borneo. His photographs have appeared in many publications, including *Life, National Geographic,* and *Sports Illustrated*. In his 2013 book *Women Who Dare,* Noble aimed his camera at women climbers. In a 2014 interview for *Adventure Journal,* Noble described how it was challenging to get some of the shots of climbers in the Black Canyon:

> To obtain them we had to borrow a six-hundred-foot length of static line, which we fixed from the top of the North Rim on the Free Nose Route. Then we rappelled in, tying the rope off strategically as we descended. When we ran out of rope we started back up with Kate and Mad climbing and me jugging above, shooting. Have you ever tried to coil six hundred feet of rope while hanging in mid-air? Believe me it's a full-body workout!

photographers and videographers. They also use stock photo agencies to market their work to publishers and media sites.

Beginning sports photographers can also enter the field working as assistants to experienced photographers or as interns for a larger publication. These positions provide on-the-job training, allowing beginners to increase their technical skills and experience, and they may lead to a full-time staff position.

PREPARING YOURSELF

There is no standard educational path for a career in sports photography or videography. People who want to work in this field should have a creative view, strong photography or video skills, and a passion for sports. Taking courses in photography, videography, and other visual arts can help a person prepare for and gain the necessary skills for this career. Other key skills to have for this career include a good knowledge of lighting, positioning and camera techniques, and experience with photo and video editing. Some people find that an intense one-year certificate program in photography or videography is a good way to gain the skills needed for this career. Others find that earning an associate's degree in photography can help them build technical skills. Often these programs offer courses in camera equipment, lighting, digital imaging, color design, and digital printing.

Before applying for a job or freelance assignment, sports photographers need a portfolio of photographs or videos that they have taken. A portfolio displays the person's talents and ability to prospective employers. To build a portfolio, candidates can take pictures or video at local sporting events, after they have obtained permissions from event organizers. Another way to build a portfolio is to take photography or videography classes at a local community college, photography studio, or private trade school.

FUTURE PROSPECTS

According to the US Bureau of Labor Statistics (BLS), jobs for all photographers, including sports photographers, is expected to grow 3 percent

At a football game, a sports photographer uses a powerful camera lens that allows him to get a close-up picture of the players from a distance.

from 2014 to 2024. This rate is slower than the average for all occupations. As the costs of digital cameras decrease, more amateur photographers are entering the field. In addition, online stock photo services provide people and businesses access to stock photographs, reducing the need to hire a sports photographer. The decline in the newspaper industry is also expected to reduce the demand for news and sports photographers to provide photographs for print. With reduced barriers to entry, sports photographers and videographers will face competition for most assignments. In addition, full-time salaried positions may be harder to find as more companies are using freelancers instead of hiring staff. As a result, sports photographers and videographers who have a variety of skills, such as the ability to edit their own images and also take digital video, will make themselves more attractive candidates to employers.

FOR MORE INFORMATION

BOOKS

Aspland, Marc, Jonny Wilkinson, and Oliver Holt. *The Art of Sports Photography*. New York, NY: Prestel, 2014.
An accomplished sports photographer, Marc Aspland presents highlights of his career documenting incredible moments in sports.

Miller, Peter Read. *Peter Read Miller on Sports Photography: A Sports Illustrated Photographer's Tips, Tricks, and Tales on Shooting Football, the Olympics, and Portraits of Athletes*. Berkeley, CA: New Riders, 2014.
The author, a *Sports Illustrated* photographer for thirty years, takes the reader behind the scenes of many of his most iconic shots, relating the stories behind the photos of some of the world's greatest athletic events, including the Olympics and the Super Bowl.

Skinner, Peter. *Sports Photography: How to Capture Action and Emotion*. New York, NY: Allworth, 2007.
Seasoned sports photographer Peter Skinner uses 211 examples from the work of several renowned sports photographers to show exactly how to take great action photos.

ORGANIZATIONS

American Society of Media Photographers
150 North 2nd Street
Philadelphia, PA 19106
(215) 451-2767
Website: http://asmp.org
The American Society of Media Photographers (ASMP) is the premier trade association for the world's most respected photographers. ASMP has nearly seven thousand members and thirty-nine chapters.

National Press Photographers Association
3200 Croasdaile Drive, Suite 306
Durham, NC 27705
(919) 383-7246
Website: https://nppa.org
The National Press Photographers Association works for the advancement of visual journalism.

Professional Photographers Association
229 Peachtree Street NE, Suite 2200
Atlanta, GA 30303
(404) 522-8600
Website: http://www.ppa.com
Professional Photographers of America (PPA) is the world's largest nonprofit photography association for professional photographers, with more than twenty-nine thousand members in more than fifty countries.

Sports Video Group
260 Fifth Avenue, Suite 600
New York, NY 10001
(212) 481-8140
Website: www.sportsvideo.org
The Sports Video Group provides support, education,
    and networking opportunities to people who work to
    create, produce, and distribute sports content.

PERIODICALS

Digital Photo
25 Braintree Hill Office Park, Suite 404
Braintree, MA 02184
(617) 706-9110
Website: http://www.dpmag.com
Digital Photo offers the latest news, equipment reviews
    and previews, and photography tips and techniques
    for digital camera users.

WEBSITES

Because of the changing nature of internet links, Rosen
Publishing has developed an online list of websites
related to the subject of this book. This site is updated
regularly. Please use this link to access this list:

http://www.rosenlinks.com/CCWC/sports

CHAPTER 2

MEDIA AND COMMUNICATION EQUIPMENT WORKER

Behind the scenes at ESPN's *Monday Night Football*, a small army of production people work to make sure the broadcast goes off without a hitch. A staff of approximately 250 to 300 people work each game, from camerapeople to technical directors. Some of these workers are media and communication equipment workers. They arrive with the crew three days before game day, bringing nine trucks full of computers and technical equipment.

They work to set up most of ESPN's twenty-eight cameras in the stadium, along with approximately

Philip Rivers, quarterback of the San Diego Chargers of the National Football League, is interviewed by a reporter after a *Monday Night Football* game at Qualcomm Stadium.

forty microphones used in each broadcast. Using these cameras and microphones, ESPN reporters can broadcast almost every on-field conversation during the game. The crew also sets up pregame and in-game lighting. During the game, media and communication workers operate and monitor the equipment, making sure that everything is working properly. If something happens, they must be ready to react and fix it.

IMPORTANT SKILLS FOR MEDIA AND COMMUNICATION WORKERS

Several skills are important for those pursuing a career as a media and communication equipment worker. Good communication skills are essential, as workers need to communicate with many coworkers and supervisors to set up equipment properly before a live sporting event. In addition, workers should have a steady hand and good hand-eye coordination when setting up equipment and cables, which often involves manipulating small knobs, dials, and other parts. Workers should be competent using computers to program equipment and edit audio and video recordings as needed. Workers in this field should also be good problem solvers and able to think quickly on their feet. When something goes wrong during a live broadcast, they need to be able to diagnose the problem and implement a solution quickly.

A DAY IN THE LIFE

Media and communication equipment workers set up, test, operate, and monitor audio, video, and digital equipment for sporting events. They also set up and operate spotlights and other lighting systems. The type of equipment they use varies according to the event. Workers can also use their technical skills for concerts, meetings and conventions, presentations, and news conferences.

On smaller events, media and communication workers often handle many tasks. On larger events, their assignments may be more specialized. Audio and video technicians set up, test, and operate audio and video equipment. They work with microphones, sound speakers, video screens, projectors, wires and cables, and sound and mixing boards at sporting and other events. They connect wires and cables to set up and operate the audio and video equipment. They may also set up and operate custom lighting systems for an event.

Sound engineering technicians operate equipment that produces or projects sound, music, and special effects at sporting events or other kinds of events. Before the event, they set up the sound equipment and test it with sound producers and other participants so that it creates the desired sound or effects. They operate transmitters to broadcast radio or television programs and use computers to operate the equipment and edit audio recordings.

Media and communication equipment workers typically perform the following tasks:

- Set up and take down equipment needed for an event
- Operate, test, and monitor audio, video, lighting, and broadcast equipment
- Record speech, music, and other sounds on recording equipment or computers
- Test and resolve any equipment issues
- Diagnose and correct any equipment or technological issues
- Coordinate audio feeds with television or other video images
- Switch video input sources from one camera to another camera
- Determine filming sequence and camera movements
- Ensure proper care, handling, and storage of equipment

Working conditions in this career vary by event. Long hours and work at night and on weekends should be expected as workers are required to be present before,

An audio technician works to set up sound equipment and test it with sound producers before a sporting event. He works to diagnose and fix any issues as they arise.

A teenager learns how to operate a video camera. Video technicians are responsible for the setup, operation, and troubleshooting of video equipment at sporting events.

during, and after sporting events. If the live event is outdoors, workers are expected to work through all types of weather conditions.

PREPARING YOURSELF

There are several ways to prepare for a career as a media and communication equipment worker. Some people attend technical school or earn an associate's degree in communication and broadcast technology. These programs offer training in radio production, television production, and digital video editing. These programs typically include hands-on experience with equipment that will be used. High school students interested in this career should take courses in math, physics, and electronics. They should also take computer classes. High school students can get experience by working in their school's audiovisual department.

Some people prepare for this career by working as an assistant for a more experienced technician already in the field and getting on-the-job training and experience. On-the-job training often includes learning how to set up cables or automation systems, testing electrical equipment, learning industry codes and standards, and following safety procedures.

Because technology is constantly changing, workers in this field are expected to keep up-to-date on the latest equipment. They can enroll in continuing education classes or get on-the-job training in new equipment and technologies. Although not required by most employers, earning a certificate will give a worker an advantage in getting a job or promotion. Earning a certificate such as a radio and television broadcasting technical certificate tells employers that the worker is keeping up with the latest industry standards and technologies.

FUTURE PROSPECTS

According to the Bureau of Labor Statistics, jobs for all media and communication occupations, including equipment workers, is expected to grow 4 percent from 2014 to 2024. This rate is slower than the average for all occupations. However, jobs for audio and visual equipment technicians is expected to grow faster, 12 percent from 2014 to 2024, as more audio and video technicians will be needed to set up new equipment or upgrade older, complex systems.

Candidates who will have the most opportunities are those who have hands-on experience with a variety of complex electronics, equipment, and software. An associate's degree in broadcast technology, broadcast production, or a related field can also improve a candidate's opportunities. Experienced workers with strong technical skills can advance to supervisory positions.

FOR MORE INFORMATION

BOOKS

Ballou, Glen. *Handbook for Sound Engineers*. 4th ed. New York, NY: Focal, 2015.
This book is a comprehensive reference guide for audio engineers.

Cape, Timothy W., and Jim Smith. *Audiovisual Best Practices: The Design and Integration Process for the AV and Construction Industries*. Fairfax, VA: International Communications Industries Association, 2005.
This book presents an overview of the industry and explores the inner workings of AV projects with start-to-finish process descriptions.

Grimes, Brad. *Networked AV Systems*. New York, NY: McGraw-Hill Education, 2014.
Featuring diagrams, photos, notes, and chapter reviews, this book provides the essential information AV and IR professionals need to know to work with network-driven equipment and processes.

Huntington, John. *Show Networks and Control Systems*. Brooklyn, NY: Zircon Designs, 2012.
This book provides an in-depth look at the control and networking technology involved in backstage

control, such as lighting, lasers, sound, special effects, and more.

White, Ira. *Audio Made Easy: Or How to Be a Sound Engineer without Really Trying*. Milwaukee, WI: Hal Leonard, 2007.
In this beginner's guide to live sound, the author presents information in an accessible and easy-to-understand format.

ORGANIZATIONS

Audio Engineering Society
551 Fifth Avenue, Suite 1225
New York, NY 10176
(212) 661-8528
Website: http://www.aes.org
The Audio Engineering Society is an international organization that unites audio engineers, creative artists, scientists, and students worldwide by promoting advances in audio and sharing new knowledge and research.

InfoComm International
(800) 659-7469
Website: http://www.infocomm.org

InfoComm International is a trade association that represents the professional audiovisual and information communications industries.

National Association of Broadcast Employees and Technicians
501 3rd Street NW
Washington, DC 20001
(202) 434-1254
Website: http://www.nabetcwa.org
The National Association of Broadcast Employees and Technicians represents more than ten thousand workers in broadcasting and related industries.

WEBSITES

Because of the changing nature of internet links, Rosen Publishing has developed an online list of websites related to the subject of this book. This site is updated regularly. Please use this link to access this list:

http://www.rosenlinks.com/CCWC/sports

CHAPTER 3

SPORTS OFFICIALS, UMPIRES, AND REFEREES

Baseball umpire Nate Tomlinson dreams of making it to the major leagues. Tomlinson's baseball dreams started years ago, when he played baseball as a child. As he got older, he loved to work as an umpire at youth games, calling balls and strikes behind the plate. In early 2010, he attended the Jim Evans Academy of Professional Umpiring, an approved professional umpire training school. At the five-week training school, students learn everything from rules to mechanics to positioning. After the training school, Tomlinson worked as an umpire in summer baseball games for college players. Today as a Class A minor league baseball umpire, Tomlinson works 140 games in about 150 days, traveling from stadium to stadium across the country.

The manager of the Trenton Thunder, an American minor league baseball team, argues with the home plate umpire after a close play at the plate.

A DAY IN THE LIFE

Sports officials make sure that the rules are followed at sporting events and the game is fair. Most competitive sports, including football, baseball, hockey, soccer, tennis, and swimming, use sports officials. Following the rules of the game, sports officials monitor player safety, track time, and assess penalties for rule violations. They typically perform the following tasks:

- Officiate sporting events and competitions, enforcing rules and assessing penalties as needed
- Judge performances in sports such as gymnastics, swimming, or diving
- Inspect sports equipment and participants to ensure player safety
- Track time in sporting events, starting and stopping play as necessary
- Settle disputes between participants

Sports officials often are on the field to get the best view of the game's action. In many sports, officials work in groups. Baseball umpires and soccer referees work this way. Each official has his or her own specific responsibilities during the game. For example, in baseball, one umpire works behind home plate to signal balls and strikes, while others work at different spots on the field. Sports officials rely on their training and knowledge of rules to make the appropriate calls and assess penalties. In some cases, sports officials use video replay to assist in making accurate calls.

Being a sports official can be a stressful job. Officials need to make quick decisions. Often, players, coaches, and fans strongly argue with their decisions. In addition, sports officials often work outdoors, in all weather conditions. The hours can be irregular, with sporting events taking place at night, on weekends, or on holidays. Sports officials may be required to travel for sporting events in other cities, states, and countries. Some sports even require officials to run, jog,

IMPORTANT QUALITIES FOR OFFICIALS

Several qualities are important for success as a sports official. First, sports officials must have good verbal communication skills. They inform players about the rules of the game and explain their decisions to players, coaches, and other officials. Sports officials should also be accurate and fast decision makers. In the middle of the game, a football referee must decide on the spot if a player was down before he fumbled the ball. A baseball umpire must decide if a pitch was a ball or a strike. As many officials work together to officiate a game, officials also should be able to work well with others. Sports officials must also be in good physical condition and have the stamina required to stand, walk, run, or squat for long periods of time during sporting events.

The home plate umpire calls strike three in a Major League Baseball game between the Colorado Rockies and the Philadelphia Phillies.

or skate throughout the game. Many sports officials work part-time and are employed in other jobs.

PREPARING YOURSELF

Each sport has different rules and procedures, and it is essential for officials to be very familiar with their sport. Sports officials must have detailed knowledge about a sport, its rules, policies, and procedures. Many people learn a sport's rules through years of playing or volunteering to officiate local youth games. Some people add to their knowledge by taking a training course or attending a clinic that teaches rules and regulations.

Each state and sporting association has its own education requirements for officials. Some states have no formal education requirement, while others require officials to have a high school diploma. Certification and training requirements also vary by sport and state. Most sports organizations require officials to be certified and/or licensed.

A hockey referee watches as players fight for the puck. If either player commits a penalty, the referee will stop play and send the player to the penalty box.

In order to earn a certification, officials need to pass an exam on the rules of the sport. Some states and associations require potential officials to attend classes before taking the exam or joining the association. For some sports, applicants must pass vision, hearing, and physical fitness tests before becoming certified. Officials may also be required to attend off-season training sessions to learn about rule changes and improve their performance. Those interested in officiating should contact the appropriate association to learn the specific requirements for their state and sport.

FUTURE PROSPECTS

Most new officials begin by volunteering to officiate youth sports. With a few years of experience, they can advance to paid positions in high school sports and later to the collegiate levels. Some officials advance through college levels to work in professional sports leagues.

According to the Bureau of Labor Statistics, jobs for umpires, referees, and other sports officials are expected to grow 5 percent from 2014 to 2024. This rate is about the same as the average for all occupations. Population increases are expected to fuel a rise in the overall number of people participating in organized sports. The addition of new school athletic programs and teams is also expected to increase participation in high school and college sports. With more people playing sports, the need for officials is also projected to increase.

At the college and professional sports level, competition for jobs is expected to be strong, with many applicants for only a few open positions. Candidates with prior officiating experience will have the best job opportunities.

FOR MORE INFORMATION

BOOKS

Ager, David. *The Soccer Referee's Manual.* New York, NY: Bloomsbury, 2016.
This book is a reference guide for soccer referees at all levels and includes FIFA's most recent Laws of the Game and guidance on how referees should administer the laws and control game play.

Austro, Ben. *So You Think You Know Football? The Armchair Ref's Guide to the Official Rules.* Lanham, MD: Taylor Trade, 2015.
This book illustrates and interprets the NFL rule book using examples from real game situations.

Stewart, Wayne. *You're the Umpire: 152 Scenarios to Test Your Baseball Knowledge.* New York, NY: Skyhorse, 2016.
This book, authored by a professional sportswriter, allows readers to test their knowledge of the game.

ORGANIZATIONS

National Association of Sports Officials
2017 Lathrop Avenue
Racine, WI 53405

(262) 632-5448

Website: http://www.naso.org/Home.aspx

The National Association of Sports Officials (NASO) is the world's largest organization for sports officials at every level and all sports. NASO advocates for sports officials and helps them maintain the highest level of officiating skills.

National Youth Sports Officials Association

2050 Vista Parkway

West Palm Beach, FL 33411

(800) 688-5437

Website: http://www.nays.org/officials

The National Youth Sports Officials Association (NYSOA) helps both veteran and beginning officials have a clear understanding of their roles and responsibilities to make a positive influence in the lives of youth.

WEBSITES

Because of the changing nature of internet links, Rosen Publishing has developed an online list of websites related to the subject of this book. This site is updated regularly. Please use this link to access this list:

http://www.rosenlinks.com/CCWC/sports

CHAPTER 4

PERSONAL TRAINER AND FITNESS INSTRUCTOR

In many gyms, a personal trainer works one-on-one with a client, demonstrating how to use the gym's weight and cardio machines or pushing the client to complete twenty-five push-ups. In another room, an aerobics instructor leads a Zumba class, demonstrating the routine and encouraging the class's thirty participants to keep their heart rates up while dancing. These fitness professionals educate and motivate clients, supporting and guiding them to improved health and fitness.

Lisa Cunningham works as a personal trainer in London. Every day on the job is different. Some

An energetic fitness instructor leads a group exercise class in a gym. She teaches the routines to class participants, while constantly motivating and encouraging them.

days she gets up early to start training clients at 6:30 a.m., while other days do not start until 10 a.m. Typically, she works three to four hours in the morning and another five hours in the late afternoon and evening. During her midday break, Cunningham works out herself and designs client programs and eating plans. Her favorite part of the job is seeing how her work can help people change physically and mentally. Although she does not enjoy the administrative side of the job, which includes preparing invoices and responding to emails, she knows that it is a necessary part of owning her own studio. Her advice to people considering a career as a personal trainer: be focused, patient, and love it.

A personal trainer works one-on-one with a client, talking him through each exercise and making sure he is using proper form and technique to avoid injury.

STRENGTH AND CONDITIONING COACHES

Like personal trainers and fitness instructors, strength and conditioning coaches work with clients to improve their fitness. The main difference is that these coaches mainly train athletes who want to improve sports performance and skills. Strength and conditioning coaches work with athletic teams at all levels, from high school to college to professional teams. They train the team as a group or individually and tailor workout programs as needed. Some strength and conditioning coaches maintain the team's weight room, keeping an inventory of equipment and recommending purchases when necessary. Strength and conditioning coaches may also develop rehabilitation routines for injured athletes.

While jobs with college and professional teams often require a minimum of a bachelor's degree, some high schools accept a strength and conditioning coach with an associate's degree in strength training or a related field. Candidates may also be required to have a professional certification and several years of experience in strength training.

A DAY IN THE LIFE

Personal trainers and fitness instructors lead, instruct, and motivate people to exercise. They work with individuals or groups in activities such as cardiovascular exercises, strength training, and flexibility stretches. They train people of all ages and fitness levels. In a typical day, they might:

- Demonstrate to clients how to perform exercises and routines
- Watch clients as they perform exercises to ensure safety
- Provide modified and alternate exercises for clients of different fitness levels and skills
- Monitor clients' fitness progress and adapt programs if necessary
- Demonstrate the proper and safe use of exercise equipment
- Provide information about nutrition and weight control to clients
- Plan routines for group exercise classes
- Prepare customized workout routines for clients to reach individual goals
- Evaluate fitness level of new clients

Group fitness instructors plan and choreograph group exercise classes. Some classes focus on cardiovascular exercise such as aerobics, dance, or spinning. Other group classes incorporate strength training with weights. Group instructors design routines and choose music. During the class, they lead routines and help participants as needed. Some specialized fitness instructors teach specific types of exercise, such as Pilates or yoga.

Personal trainers generally work one-on-one with individual clients or small groups of clients. When working with a new client, a personal trainer evaluates the client's current fitness level and goals. Then, he or she designs a custom workout routine for each client. Many personal trainers work for a gym, providing services to gym members for an additional fee. Other personal trainers work for themselves, taking on clients and providing services in their clients' homes. Over a period of time, the trainer evaluates the client's progress and adjusts workout routines as needed.

A personal trainer meets with a new client at a gym and discusses the client's fitness goals. With this information, the trainer can create a workout plan for the client.

PREPARING YOURSELF

The education and training for personal trainers and fitness instructors varies by specialty and hiring facility. Almost all personal trainers and instructors have a high school diploma. Many also have an associate's degree in a health or fitness field such as kinesiology or physical education. In school, candidates can take classes in nutrition, exercise technique, biology, anatomy, and group fitness to prepare for this career. They should also study how to develop fitness programs for people of different ages and fitness levels.

In addition to education requirements, most employers require personal trainers and fitness instructors to be certified before they begin working with members at a gym or health club. Students can earn certifications in cardio-pulmonary resuscitation (CPR) and automated external defibrillators. They can also earn certificates with national organizations such as the National Federation of Personal Trainers, the American Council on Exercise, or the National Academy of Sports Medicine. Certificate programs train students to design and manage fitness programs. Students learn the science of exercise, basic physiology, conditioning, strength, injury prevention, and safety. They also learn how to assess and motivate personal training clients. Certification generally lasts two years, and students are required to complete continuing education courses in order to renew their certification.

FUTURE PROSPECTS

With experience, personal trainers and fitness instructors may advance to a head trainer or instructor position. In this role, they will be responsible for hiring and overseeing a health club's staff of personal trainers and fitness instructors. They may also be responsible for attracting new personal training clients to the facility. Head trainers may also choose the facility's equipment, weights, and fitness machines. Some personal trainers and fitness instructors with experience can advance to management positions in a health club or fitness center. Although a four-year college degree is not required, candidates who earn a bachelor's degree in exercise science, physical education, or a related subject often have the best opportunities to advance into management positions. Some personal trainers and fitness instructors decide to open their own fitness facilities.

According to the Bureau of Labor Statistics, jobs for personal trainers and fitness instructors are expected to grow 8 percent from 2014 to 2024. This rate is about the same as the average for all occupations. As more people recognize the benefits of health and fitness programs to fight obesity and encourage healthy lifestyles, the demand for trainers and instructors is expected to grow. In addition, as the baby boom generation ages, many will turn to health clubs, trainers, and instructors to remain active and prevent age-related injury and illness. Personal trainers and fitness instructors who are certified or have an associate's or bachelor's degree in a health or fitness field are expected to have the best job opportunities.

FOR MORE INFORMATION

BOOKS

American Council on Exercise. *ACE Personal Trainer Manual: The Ultimate Resource for Fitness Professionals.* 4th ed. San Diego, CA: American Council on Exercise, 2010.
This book covers how to assess each client's current level of health and physical fitness and then develop a safe and effective fitness program.

Delavier, Frederic. *Strength Training Anatomy.* 3rd ed. Champaign, IL: Human Kinetics, 2010.
The more than six hundred full-color illustrations in this book reveal how muscles perform during strength exercises.

National Academy of Sports Medicine. *NASM Essentials of Personal Fitness Training.* 4th ed. Burlington, MA: Jones & Bartlett Learning, 2013.
This book is a recommended resource for NASM certified personal trainer (CPT) certification and provides a comprehensive resource for aspiring personal trainers and other health and fitness professionals.

ORGANIZATIONS

Aerobics and Fitness Association of America (AFAA)
AFAA Headquarters
1750 E. Northrop Boulevard, Suite 200
Chandler, AZ 85286-1744
(800) 446-2322
Website: http://www.afaa.com
For over thirty years, the Aerobics and Fitness
    Association of America (AFAA) has been dedicated to
    certifying group and personal trainers dedicated to
    leading others to a love for fitness and working out.

American Council on Exercise
4851 Paramount Drive
San Diego, CA 92123
(888) 825-3636
Website: https://www.acefitness.org
The American Council on Exercise is a nonprofit fitness
    certification, education, and training provider with
    more than fifty-eight thousand certified professionals.

National Federation of Professional Trainers (NFPT)
PO Box 4579
Lafayette, IN 47903
(800) 729-6378
Website: https://www.nfpt.com
The National Federation of Professional Trainers (NFPT)
has been certifying fitness professionals since 1988
and offers a certified personal trainer (CPT) program
that is accredited by the National Commission for
Certifying Agencies (NCCA).

WEBSITES

Because of the changing nature of internet links, Rosen
Publishing has developed an online list of websites
related to the subject of this book. This site is updated
regularly. Please use this link to access this list:

http://www.rosenlinks.com/CCWC/sports

CHAPTER 5

FITNESS DIRECTOR

On any given day, the fitness director at a gym or health club works to make sure everything runs smoothly. From scheduling personal trainers to organizing continuing education for club staff, a fitness director oversees all aspects and operations of a gym or health club.

A DAY IN THE LIFE

A fitness director leads the fitness staff at a gym or health club and oversees all of the facility's exercise programs. Fitness directors hire, train, and evaluate fitness staff, including personal trainers

The fitness director oversees the day-to-day operations of a gym, making sure that the fitness equipment is working properly and gym members are satisfied with their membership.

and group instructors. Fitness directors also schedule client sessions, create workout incentive programs, and organize group exercise programs. They handle administrative duties such as creating budgets and collecting member dues. Fitness directors lead new member orientations and conduct fitness assessments. They research and buy safe equipment for their gym. As many directors started their careers as personal trainers, many continue to offer training sessions or lead exercise classes.

Larger clubs may have several directors, each of whom oversees a specific area of the club. Smaller clubs may have only one director, who is responsible for the entire operation. Fitness directors typically perform the following duties:

- Manage the group exercise and personal training staff
- Train new employees and provide ongoing training for all group exercise and personal training staff
- Coordinate group exercise schedule and instructors

The gym's fitness director completes paperwork to sign up new gym members. He explains the gym's policies and takes the new members on an orientation tour of the facility.

- Establish, monitor, and analyze group budgets for group exercise and personal training
- Develop and implement policies and procedures for the fitness department
- Answer questions or resolve members' problems regarding group exercise and personal training
- Evaluate the effectiveness of the facility's exercise programs, including revenue, participation, and member satisfaction

Fitness directors use their knowledge of a club's fitness and personal training programs to generate sales for the club. They carry out promotions to increase membership and sell personal training services to new members. They also ensure that current customers are satisfied with the club.

PREPARING YOURSELF

At a minimum, people who want to work as fitness directors should have high school diplomas. In some cases, employers prefer candidates who have an associate's or bachelor's degree in exercise-related fields.

Fitness directors need to be experts in exercise and physiology. Many directors begin their careers working as personal trainers or group exercise instructors. In these roles, they learn about physical exercise, nutrition, and the

GENE DENOTA: TRAINING AND EXERCISE DIRECTOR

In his role as the training and exercise director for the Darien YMCA in Darien, Connecticut, Gene DeNota supervises and oversees the quality and implementation of all personal training and group exercise classes at his club. He works with other directors at the YMCA to ensure that all members have a smooth and enjoyable experience. In addition, DeNota continues to lead personal training sessions with clients and group exercise classes. He designs workout programs and meets with clients to talk about their fitness goals. To prepare for this career, DeNota obtained several health and fitness certifications. He also earned an associate's degree in individual studies from Westchester Community College in New York.

human body. Students interested in this career can prepare by taking classes in nutrition, health, exercise science, and other health-related topics. Business and communication classes can also be beneficial, especially if the student hopes to advance to positions with more responsibility.

Eligible candidates should also hold a personal training certification from an accredited organization, such as the American Council on Exercise (ACE), the American College

of Sports Medicine (ACSM), and the National Academy of Sports Medicine (NASM). In addition, fitness directors should be certified in cardiopulmonary resuscitation (CPR).

To earn one of these certifications, candidates will have to pass a test that examines their knowledge of fitness assessment, program design, anatomy, physiology, and nutrition. Earning several certifications in a variety of exercise and training fields can open up more opportunities and show employers that a candidate is serious about keeping up with the latest training techniques, equipment, and programs.

FUTURE PROSPECTS

As the US population grows and ages, the demand for fitness facilities is expected to increase. As more people use health clubs and gyms, the demand for fitness workers, including fitness directors, will also rise.

An instructor demonstrates cardiopulmonary resuscitation (CPR) to gym staff on a dummy. After completing the class, each member of the staff will earn their certification in CPR.

While the BLS does not provide employment figures specific to fitness directors, it does predict that jobs for personal trainers and fitness instructors are expected to grow 8 percent from 2014 to 2024. This rate is about the same as the average for all occupations. This growth in the fitness industry could signal a favorable outlook for fitness director positions.

FOR MORE INFORMATION

BOOKS

American Council on Exercise. *ACE Personal Trainer Manual: The Ultimate Resource for Fitness Professionals.* 4th ed. San Diego, CA: American Council on Exercise, 2010.
This book covers how to assess each client's current level of health and physical fitness and then develop a safe and effective fitness program.

Coffman, Sandy. *Successful Programs for Fitness and Health Clubs: 101 Profitable Ideas.* Champaign, IL: Human Kinetics, 2007.
This book presents more than one hundred ready-to-use programs for fitness centers, group exercise studios, pools, gyms, and classrooms, all designed to get hundreds of new members involved immediately.

National Academy of Sports Medicine. *NASM Essentials of Personal Fitness Training.* 4th ed. Burlington, MA: Jones & Bartlett Learning, 2013.
This book is a recommended resource for NASM certified personal trainer (CPT) certification and provides a comprehensive resource for aspiring personal trainers and other health and fitness professionals.

ORGANIZATIONS

Aerobics and Fitness Association of America (AFAA)
AFAA Headquarters
1750 E. Northrop Boulevard, Suite 200
Chandler, AZ 85286-1744
(800) 446-2322
Website: http://www.afaa.com
For over thirty years, the Aerobics and Fitness
    Association of America (AFAA) has been dedicated to
    certifying group and personal trainers dedicated to
    leading others to a love for fitness and working out.

American Council on Exercise
4851 Paramount Drive
San Diego, CA 92123
(888) 825-3636
Website: https://www.acefitness.org
The American Council on Exercise is a nonprofit fitness
    certification, education, and training provider with
    more than fifty-eight thousand certified professionals.

National Federation of Professional Trainers (NFPT)
NFPT Headquarters
PO Box 4579
Lafayette, IN 47903
(800) 729-6378
Website: https://www.nfpt.com
National Federation of Professional Trainers (NFPT) has been certifying fitness professionals since 1988 and offers a certified personal trainer (CPT) program that is accredited by the National Commission for Certifying Agencies (NCCA).

WEBSITES

Because of the changing nature of internet links, Rosen Publishing has developed an online list of websites related to the subject of this book. This site is updated regularly. Please use this link to access this list:

http://www.rosenlinks.com/CCWC/sports

CHAPTER 6

EQUIPMENT MANAGER

Some careers in sports take employees onto the field, close to the action and the athletes. Daniel Deming is the assistant sports equipment manager for D.C. United, an American professional soccer club based in Washington, DC. On a daily basis, Deming works closely with the soccer team's players and staff. As an equipment manager, Deming is responsible for the team's equipment. Before practice, he sets up practice gear in each player's locker, pumps up balls, and sets up the day's drills on the field. After practice, Deming collects the players' practice gear, washes it, and gets it ready for the next day. He keeps the players' lounge stocked with snacks like bagels, bananas, and cereal in case the

The team equipment manager orders and maintains the red uniforms for this soccer team, along with necessary equipment and supplies for the team's games and practices.

players want to eat before or after practice. When the team travels for a game, Deming and the team's other equipment managers pack twenty-five to thirty-five bags of equipment for each trip. Deming even prints player jerseys at the stadium and orders gear for each season. Although the days can be long, Deming loves his job and the experiences he is gaining in the position.

A DAY IN THE LIFE

Sports equipment managers have an important role in the daily operation of a sports team. They maintain, order, and take inventory of athletic equipment and apparel. Equipment managers do everything from fitting football shoulder pads and sharpening hockey skates to washing the team's uniforms. Each day, equipment managers make sure the team's equipment is working properly. They inspect and clean each piece to make sure it meets safety standards. They perform repairs and adjustments as needed. They also keep an inventory of equipment and organize it for storage. They choose and purchase equipment for the team. They stay up-to-date on the latest equipment and the current league rules involving uniforms, equipment, and game-day procedures.

An equipment manager for the New York Giants of the National Football League tests a radio system in quarterback helmets before Super Bowl XLVI against the New England Patriots.

The majority of equipment managers across the country work for high school, collegiate, and professional teams. In a typical week, a sports equipment manager may perform the following tasks:

- Oversee the coordination of day-to-day sports activities and the maintenance of sports facilities

DEFLATEGATE

In 2015, the National Football League's football tampering scandal at the AFC Championship Game, better known as Deflategate, highlighted the role of equipment managers in sports. The controversy involved allegations that the New England Patriots had tampered with footballs in the game against the Indianapolis Colts. According to NFL rules, all footballs are to be inflated to a specific pressure. The pressure of the Patriots footballs, when measured by officials at halftime, was found to be less than the required pressure. When video of a Patriots equipment manager taking a bag of footballs into the bathroom before the game was found, questions arose as to whether or not he tampered with the balls to reduce their pressure, making them easier for the Patriots quarterback to grip. The entire scandal demonstrated the importance of the role of an equipment manager, making sure that the team's equipment meets rules and safety standards.

- Establish and maintain inventories of equipment and uniforms
- Determine needs and purchase sports equipment
- Coordinate all game-day equipment preparations and setup for games
- Ensure that all uniforms and equipment are maintained in a clean and usable condition

An important part of the job is ensuring that players have the right equipment to play. Sports equipment managers determine what equipment and uniforms the team needs and order it. When the equipment and uniforms arrive, they make sure they fit each player properly. If a helmet or skate does not fit, it can cause the player discomfort, reduce mobility, impair vision or hearing, and even cause injury.

Equipment managers work directly with coaches, athletic directors, team staff, and players. In order to work well with people from different backgrounds, having good communication skills and management skills is essential for this job.

PREPARING YOURSELF

While some equipment manager positions require a bachelor's degree, others will hire qualified candidates who have a high school diploma or GED combined with at least five years of experience in athletic equipment management.

While in high school, students can prepare for this career by taking classes in computer science, mathematics, and business. These courses will help students learn to handle equipment budgets and negotiate contracts. Students can also volunteer to serve as the equipment manager for a high school athletic team to gain valuable on-the-job experience.

Although certification is not a requirement to be an equipment manager, it can help a candidate stand out from a pool of applicants. The Athletic Equipment Managers Association (AEMA) offers a professional certification program for equipment managers. To earn this certification, managers must be twenty-one years old and a member in good standing with the AEMA. Managers must

Players celebrate with the team equipment manager after a game. Behind the scenes, the equipment manager must be extremely organized in order for everything to run smoothly during the season.

take and pass a certification exam. Once certified, managers take continuing education workshops and seminars to keep up-to-date on the latest developments in the field.

Several skills are also critical to success as an equipment manager. Equipment managers must be very organized, willing to work hard, and be able to get along with people from different backgrounds. Football equipment managers with big collegiate programs or professional teams can work between seventy and eighty hours a week during the season. "Most importantly you need to be excellent at multitasking because you really don't know what each day is going to bring," advises Deming. "You also need to be hard working, efficient, a quick learner and able to work long hours. Being personable sure helps, and able to mesh with a lot of different guys from different backgrounds from all over the world, especially in sports like soccer and baseball."

FUTURE PROSPECTS

High schools, colleges, and professional sports teams hire equipment managers. Most equipment managers start at the bottom and work their way up through the ranks. Entry-level positions may involve simple tasks like doing laundry. With experience, managers may earn greater responsibilities, such as fitting gear, ordering equipment, and budgeting.

Some equipment managers can be promoted to supervisory positions, managing a team of equipment managers, or administrative positions within an athletic department. Because of their contacts with sporting goods companies, sometimes equipment managers have opportunities to take jobs with those companies. As the number of sports teams increases, there will be more opportunities for qualified equipment managers in the future, particularly for collegiate and women's teams.

FOR MORE INFORMATION

BOOKS

Athletic Equipment Managers Association. *Athletic Equipment Managers Certification Manual.* Ithaca, NY: MAG, Inc., 2014.

A publication of the Athletic Equipment Managers Association (AEMA), this book is designed to help readers study for the AEMA certification exam.

Falk, Jon, and Dan Ewald. *If These Walls Could Talk: Michigan Football Stories from Inside the Big House.* Chicago, IL: Triumph Books, 2011.

Written by the equipment manager for the University of Michigan football team, this book is full of stories from inside the team's locker room.

Jacobs, Greg. *The Everything Kids' Football Book: All-Time Greats, Legendary Teams, and Today's Favorite Players—With Tips on Playing Like a Pro.* Avon, MA: Adams Media, 2014.

This book includes a chapter on the responsibilities of a football equipment manager and other behind-the-scenes roles in football.

ORGANIZATIONS

Athletic Equipment Managers Association (AEMA)
c/o Sam Trusner
207 E. Bodman
Bement, IL 61813
(217) 678-1004
Website: http://AEMA works to promote, advance, and
improve the profession of equipment management.
It works to bring about equipment improvement
for the greater safety of all participants in sports
and recreation.

WEBSITES

Because of the changing nature of internet links, Rosen
Publishing has developed an online list of websites
related to the subject of this book. This site is updated
regularly. Please use this link to access this list:

http://www.rosenlinks.com/CCWC/sports

CHAPTER 7

SCOUT

It's a hot July afternoon at Canal Park in northeast Ohio. Players from the Double-A Aeros baseball club slowly move from the clubhouse to the field for batting practice. The park is fairly quiet, as the players, coaches, and managers prepare for that night's game. A handful of people settle into seats in the stands, watching each player as they practice. They are baseball's pro scouts, learning everything they can about the players who hope to make it to the big leagues one day. The scouts take detailed notes for their player scouting reports. After following a player

A scout greets a catching prospect during instructional league workouts during the baseball offseason. The scout has studied the player to evaluate his athletic potential.

for several days at practice and during games, the scouts fill out a standard form that goes to the team's scouting director and general manager. They score each player and write verbal descriptions of their physical appearance, size, demeanor, and play. Once the report is complete, they move on to scout the next player.

A DAY IN THE LIFE

A sports or athletic scout is a person who helps college and professional teams find the best athletes in the world. Scouts travel around the state, country, and world to watch athletes perform. They evaluate the athletic ability and potential of amateur and professional players. They also monitor news sources for information about athletes, attend games, and talk to coaches about promising athletes. Scouts study game film and statistics to learn more about athletes and determine their potential. Scouts can be self-employed or work for a college, professional team, or scouting organization. A scout's job typically involves:

- Reading newspapers and other news sources to find athletes to consider
- Attending games, viewing videotapes of the athletes' performances, and studying statistics about the athletes to determine talent and potential

Prior to a game, a coach points out specific players on his baseball team to a scout who will be watching the game and evaluating players.

- Talking to athletes and coaches to see if the athlete has what it takes to succeed
- Reporting to the coach, manager, or owner of the team for which he or she is scouting
- Arranging for and offering incentives to prospective players

DATA ANALYTICS AT THE NFL DRAFT

In years past, NFL scouts evaluated players based on their eyes and ears and a "gut feeling" about a player's potential. In 2015, more teams turned to cold, hard numbers as part of their evaluation process. At the 2015 National Football League (NFL) draft, several teams combined traditional scouting and data analytics to evaluate and select new players. Data analytics is the science of examining raw data in order to draw conclusions about that data. To use data analytics, teams gathered player-performance data statistics. They analyzed results from the NFL's scouting combine, where NFL prospects run, throw, jump, and lift weights for NFL coaches, managers, and scouts. Using this information, they ranked each prospect and predicted his success in the NFL. According to Mike Tannenbaum, the football operations executive vice president for the Miami Dolphins, the Dolphins are one team that uses data analytics to help evaluate players. The Dolphins use data analytics to support what scouts see and hear when observing players. When the conclusions drawn from data do not match the scouting reports, the team digs deeper to understand why.

The baseball scout's busy season falls between March and November. During spring training, the regular season, and fall ball, a baseball scout may attend 200 live games and watch another 150 or more on hotel televisions. Because many events take place outdoors, scouts are expected to work in all weather conditions. During their busy season, scouts work long hours, including evenings and weekends. Although the idea of travel appeals to some people, scouts often make sacrifices in their personal lives and are frequently away from home because of the job's travel schedule.

PREPARING YOURSELF

People who become sports scouts are usually very passionate about a sport. They must have a good eye to identify talent, a skill that usually comes from playing or coaching the sport for several years. Although some employers, such as colleges, may require scouts to hold bachelor's degrees, many organizations require a candidate only to have a high school diploma. Often, an in-depth knowledge of the sport is more important than a formal education. Scouts should also have an eye for detail and strong interpersonal skills to develop relationships with players, coaches, and other scouts. To prepare for a career as a sports scout, students can take classes in mathematics, statistics, and business.

For those who choose to pursue an associate's or bachelor's degree, programs in physical education, sports management, nutrition, and other sports-related fields are preferred.

Many people start in this career as a part-time or volunteer scout. Once they have gained experience at that level, they can advance to paying jobs as regional scouts or assistants to regional scouts. Over time, one could advance to become a head scout for a region or a team, managing other scouts.

Sometimes, knowing the right person can lead to a scouting job. Networking within the scouting world is a great way to prepare for this career and can lead to future job opportunities. Students who spend a summer working with a local coach or scout, even to run errands, can make valuable contacts for the future.

FUTURE PROSPECTS

Because competitive athletic programs help colleges recruit students and encourage alumni donations, colleges are increasingly turning to scouts to find the most talented high school athletes. According to the Bureau of Labor Statistics, jobs for athletic coaches and scouts are expected to grow 6 percent from 2014 to 2024. This rate is about the same as the range of averages for all occupations. As participation in high school and college sports increases, the demand for coaches and scouts is also expected to increase. Many small, Division III colleges are adding new athletic teams to promote schools and recruit students. In addition, the growth in women's sports creates a need for more college scouts. Job prospects for this career should be good, although strong competition is expected for higher-paying jobs at colleges and with professional teams.

FOR MORE INFORMATION

BOOKS

Bodet, Gib. *Gib Bodet, Major League Scout: Twelve Thousand Baseball Games and Six Million Miles.* Jefferson, NC: McFarland & Co., 2014.

In this memoir, Bodet recalls humorous stories about people he worked with and describes his role in drafting and signing such players as Mike Piazza, Eric Karros, Todd Hollingsworth, Paul Konerko, Matt Kemp, Clayton Kershaw, and Chad Billingsley.

Calvin, Michael. *The Nowhere Men: The Unknown Story of Football's True Talent Spotters.* London, England: Random House UK, 2013.

In this book, award-winning sportswriter Michael Calvin explores the world of Britain's soccer scouts.

Genovese, George. *A Scout's Report: My 70 Years in Baseball.* Jefferson, NC: McFarland & Co., 2015.

His autobiography describes George Genovese's seven decades as a baseball scout.

ORGANIZATIONS

MLB Scouting Bureau
MLB Advanced Media, L.P.
75 Ninth Avenue, 5th Floor

New York, NY 10011

(866) 800-1275

Website: http://mlb.mlb.com/careers/index.
jsp?loc=mlbsb

The Major League Baseball Scouting Bureau (MLBSB) is a
centralized scouting organization within the Office of
the Baseball Commissioner.

National Scouting Report

128 Total Solutions Way

Alabaster, AL 35007

(800) 354-0072

Website: http://www.nsr-inc.com

National Scouting Report is one of the best-known high
school scouting and college recruiting organizations
in the world.

WEBSITES

Because of the changing nature of internet links, Rosen
Publishing has developed an online list of websites
related to the subject of this book. This site is updated
regularly. Please use this link to access this list:

http://www.rosenlinks.com/CCWC/sports

CHAPTER 8

SPORTS COACH OR INSTRUCTOR

Each day in the summer of 2015, Ben Shapiro rose early and headed to the Whippoorwill Club in Armonk, New York. A member of the University of Rochester tennis team, Shapiro worked as a tennis pro at the club. For about thirty to forty hours a week, he taught tennis lessons, along with another ten to twenty hours of court and facility maintenance and paperwork.

As a tennis pro, Shapiro works with players of many different abilities. Some have many years of experience, while others are raw beginners, who have never picked up a tennis racket before.

A tennis pro gives detailed instructions to a beginning player about how to hold a racket and the proper position when hitting the ball.

When teaching young kids, Shapiro says that his job is to make sure they have fun on the court, while playing games that improve hand-eye coordination and other basic tennis skills. According to Shapiro, one of the best perks of his job is that it allows him to be outside on the tennis court for most of the day. However, he admits that being on his feet and teaching for hours at a time, day after day, can be physically demanding.

A DAY IN THE LIFE

Sport coaches and instructors, like Shapiro, teach athletes what they need to know to be successful at a sport. They help beginners learn the basic rules, techniques, grips, and movement of a sport. They also work with experienced athletes to help them improve their skills and take their game to the next level. While instructors work with individual students or small groups, coaches often work with an entire team. Coaches and sports instructors typically perform the following duties:

- Plan, organize, and conduct practice sessions
- Analyze the strengths and weaknesses of individual athletes
- Plan and direct physical conditioning programs
- Instruct athletes on proper techniques, game strategies, sportsmanship, and the rules of the sport

A ski instructor gives direction to skiers during a private lesson before skiing together down the mountain. The instructor teaches students of all skill levels, from beginning to advanced.

- Keep records of athletes' performance
- Provide strategies, direction, encouragement, and motivation to prepare athletes for games
- Call plays and make decisions about strategy during games
- Identify and recruit potential athletes

The life of a coach or sports instructor varies by the type of sport and the level of the athletes involved. For example, a ski instructor at a Colorado resort will have very different responsibilities and duties from a club soccer coach. Despite their day-to-day differences, all coaches and sports instructors are teachers. They need to have a lot of knowledge about their sport, its rules, and strategies. Coaches and instructors must be able to communicate their knowledge to their students effectively, so that they can understand and apply it. They must also be good motivators, able to get the best out of the athletes they work with.

Coaches develop strategies for athletes to be successful in competition. They prepare athletes for a game, match, or meet. During the event, coaches give instruction to their teams and athletes. Some coaches also recruit players for the team.

Sports coaches and instructors are always learning about their sport and how to teach more effectively. Many are members of professional organizations of coaches and

During a gymnastics camp, a gymnastics coach assists a young student with a handstand on the balance beam and moves her legs into the proper position.

instructors. Many also attend clinics and seminars to keep up-to-date on the latest equipment, rule changes, and developments in their sport.

PREPARING YOURSELF

Coaches and sports instructors come from a variety of backgrounds, from ex-athletes to fans, but all have a passion for teaching the sport. Some high schools and most colleges require coaches and coaching assistants to have a bachelor's degree. For other coaching and sports instructor positions, there is no education requirement. While in high school, students can take classes in biology, health, and physical education to prepare for this career.

Whether they play it themselves at a high level or can explain how to play it effectively to others, coaches and instructors have a solid understanding of their sport and its rules and strategies. Students interested in this career should try to get as much experience as possible in their sport. They can participate as a player, manager, trainer, or in intramural leagues.

To get started in coaching, students can get experience volunteering with a club or school team. Students can also get coaching experience by working as an assistant to a more experienced coach, learning on-the-job about coaching

CARLOS GANCEDO, SKI INSTRUCTOR

The day begins when the alarm goes off at 6:45 a.m. First coffee and breakfast, then Carlos Gancedo heads to work as a ski instructor in Aspen, Colorado. If there is at least six inches (fifteen centimeters) of snow on the ground, Gancedo knows that it is going to be a good day. He grabs his ski boots from the locker room and heads out to meet his first client of the day. As a ski instructor, he meets a variety of people of all ages, from all around the world. He spends most of the afternoon skiing with clients, finding runs that they like. During the peak ski season, he can work thirty days in a row, without a day off. After the day's skiing is complete, Gancedo meets up with clients and other ski instructors to mingle and socialize. Then he heads home to relax, catch up on errands, and watch a little television. The next day, he heads out to the slopes again. Gancedo warns that the life of a ski instructor isn't for everyone, but if a person is passionate about skiing, it might just be the perfect fit!

styles and skills and what it takes to be a head coach. Many communities have sporting programs such as Little League or recreational basketball. Students can get experience volunteering in these programs as coaches, umpires, or referees.

Some organizations require coaches and sports instructors to be certified. Students should check with organizations for their sport to see if there are any certification requirements and how to become certified.

FUTURE PROSPECTS

Coaches and sports instructors work for high schools, colleges, professional teams, youth leagues, summer camps, recreation centers, and sporting clubs. Some work directly for individual athletes. According to the Bureau of Labor Statistics, jobs for athletic coaches are expected to grow 6 percent from 2014 to 2024. This rate is about the same as the average for all occupations. As Americans continue to pursue interests in sports and physical fitness, the need for coaches and sports instructors will continue to increase. Today, health clubs and recreation centers hire instructors and coaches to teach sports from tennis and golf to scuba diving and snowboarding. Those candidates with the most training and experience will have the best opportunities. In addition, the expansion of high school, college, and professional sports will create new opportunities, although competition for these positions will be strong.

The advancement opportunities for sports instructors and coaches depend on their skills and results. Success is often measured by the number of students and their level of play. Successful instructors and coaches may open their own schools or camps or write instructional books. Successful coaches at lower levels may be hired to lead bigger programs.

FOR MORE INFORMATION

BOOKS

Henry, Ran. *Spurrier: How the Ball Coach Taught the South to Play Football.* Guilford, CT: Lyons Press, 2014.
A biography of Steve Spurrier, the 1966 Heisman Trophy winner and NFL quarterback who became a coach and turned three universities into winners.

ORGANIZATIONS

American Baseball Coaches Association (ABCA)
4101 Piedmont Parkway, Suite C
Greensboro, NC 27410
Website: http://www.abca.org/landing/index
The ABCA is the primary professional organization for baseball coaches at the amateur level. Association membership includes coaches in eight divisions.

American Football Coaches Association (AFCA)
100 Legends Lane
Waco, TX 76706
(254) 754-9900
Website: http://www.afca.com

The AFCA works to provide education, interaction, and networking in order to achieve personal and professional development for the American football coaching profession. More than eleven thousand coaches nationwide belong to the AFCA.

National Youth Sports Coaches Association (NYSCA)
2050 Vista Parkway
West Palm Beach, FL 33411
(800) 688-5437
Website: http://www.nays.org/coaches
Part of the National Alliance for Youth Sports, the National Youth Sports Coaches Association (NYSCA) is the most widely used coach training program in the nation.

WEBSITES

Because of the changing nature of internet links, Rosen Publishing has developed an online list of websites related to the subject of this book. This site is updated regularly. Please use this link to access this list:

http://www.rosenlinks.com/CCWC/sports

CHAPTER 9

SALES REPRESENTATIVE

Peope who want to work in sports find that working in sales offers many career opportunities. Sales representatives, also known as sales associates or salespeople, work in many different areas of the sports arena. At the stadium complex, sales associates work in retail stores and food service establishments. Sales representatives can also work for a sports team directly, working at the ticket office to sell individual game tickets to fans or in the office selling season tickets, seat licenses, and corporate luxury boxes. Other sales representatives work for sporting goods stores, selling merchandise to customers or for companies selling products to stores. In all of these jobs, sales representatives interact with customers, help them pick

A sales associate straightens a display of athletic shoes so that the store's customers can easily compare shoe styles and select a pair to purchase.

Sales associates prepare a visually appealing display of New Balance and Saucony running shoes, two of the world's largest suppliers of athletic shoes and apparel.

the right product, and encourage them to buy. In order to succeed in this role, sales representatives must have excellent communication skills and customer service skills, along with the ability to deal with a variety of personality types.

A DAY IN THE LIFE

Retail sales representatives who work in stadium shops or sporting goods stores interact directly with customers. They greet customers as they enter a store and answer any questions they might have about the merchandise. Sales associates help customers choose and fit equipment such as hockey goalie leg pads or baseball cleats. They demonstrate sporting gear and equipment such as treadmills or weight machines. To do this effectively, they must have an in-depth knowledge of the prod-

TICKET SALES REPRESENTATIVE

A ticket sales representative offers tickets to interested buyers to fill the seats at a sporting event. They may sell tickets to individuals, groups, or companies.

Sales jobs are also available in the ticket office of a professional sports team. Ticket sales representatives market and sell tickets for a sports team. They might work in the box office on game day, selling individual tickets to fans. They might also work in the office, calling leads to sell ticket packages, luxury suites, and special group and corporate packages. The sales representative may receive some leads for potential sales from others in the sales department, but they are usually expected to generate their own leads. They spend much of the day on the phone, calling potential customers and following up on leads. People who work in this career need to have strong interpersonal and communication skills in order to communicate effectively with coworkers and customers.

ucts sold in their store. In addition to selling items, retail sales associates may also be responsible for ringing up customers at a cash register, packaging purchased items, preparing sales contracts for larger purchases, and maintaining sales records. They also restock shelves with products, unpack deliveries from suppliers, and inventory the store's products. Retail sales associates typically work indoors but often spend hours on their feet, walking around the store. Depending on the store's hours, a sales associate may be required to work evenings and weekends. Because the holiday shopping season is one of the busiest times for retail stores, retail sales associates often have to work long hours during the holiday season.

Sales associates generally perform the following tasks, although duties depend on the type of job and product being sold:

- Greet customers and offer assistance
- Recommend merchandise to customers
- Explain the use of merchandise to customers, answer questions, and demonstrate products as needed
- Ring up customer purchases at cash register and package as necessary
- Restock shelves as needed
- Unpack deliveries and organize stockroom and/or warehouse
- Create merchandise displays to encourage sales
- Prepare sales reports
- Inventory store merchandise

Some sales representatives work directly for a sporting goods company or brand. Instead of selling to individual consumers, they sell a company's products or services to schools, stores, and other organizations. For example, Upstart Sports is a company that distributes sports products from a variety of family-owned companies. The company works with sales professionals to sell sporting goods to high schools, colleges, youth leagues, training facilities, and other organizations.

PREPARING YOURSELF

Most retail sales positions do not have an education requirement, although some employers prefer employees who have earned a high school diploma. Instead of a four-year degree, many employers will accept related sales work experience. Many retailers provide on-the-job training for new employees. The training can last from a few days to a few months and varies by the type of store and merchandise being sold. For example, sales associates selling sports equipment will receive different instruction from those selling game-day shirts. During training, new employees learn company guidelines, safety procedures, and customer service standards. To prepare for this career, students can take classes in business, accounting, and communications.

FUTURE PROSPECTS

According to the Bureau of Labor Statistics, employment of retail sales workers, including sports retail sales, is projected to grow 7 percent from 2014 to 2024. This rate is about as fast as the average for all occupations. Because turnover is frequently high in retail sales positions, there are often many job openings.

As sales associates gain experience, they often take on greater responsibility and may get to choose the department where they will work. Advancement can also lead to raises and higher commissions. After many years of experience, sales representatives can advance into supervisory and management positions, although some employers require a bachelor's degree for management positions or require candidates to complete a management training program.

FOR MORE INFORMATION

BOOKS

Mullin, Bernard, Stephen Hardy, and William Sutton. *Sport Marketing*. 4th ed. Champlain, IL: Human Kinetics, 2014.
This book explores how fans, players, coaches, media, and companies interact to drive the sports industry.

Reyhle, Nicole, and Jason Prescott. *Retail 101: The Guide to Managing and Marketing Your Retail Business*. Columbus, OH: McGraw-Hill, 2014.
This book is a hands-on, practical guide for those working in or owning a retail business.

Walkup, Renee P. *Selling to Anyone Over the Phone*. New York, NY: American Management Association, 2011.
This book is full of tips and techniques for making sales over the phone.

ORGANIZATIONS

National Retail Federation (NRF)
1101 New York Avenue NW
Washington, DC 20005
(800) 673-4692
Website: https://nrf.com

NRF is the world's largest retail trade association, representing retailers from the United States and more than forty-five countries.

WEBSITES

Because of the changing nature of internet links, Rosen Publishing has developed an online list of websites related to the subject of this book. This site is updated regularly. Please use this link to access this list:

http://www.rosenlinks.com/CCWC/sports

CHAPTER 10
WEBSITE DEVELOPER

Almost every company and organization today has a website. Even athletes and celebrities have websites. Customers visit a company's website to learn more about products, find store locations, and buy products online. Fans visit team and athlete websites to get information about upcoming games, promotions, and appearances. Designing a website that is creative and attractive to customers and fans is the job of web developers. For someone who enjoys both computers and sports, this job may be the perfect combination!

A website designer works with a tablet and desktop computer to design a site for a client. Designers can create personalized sites for athletes, teams, companies, and others.

A DAY IN THE LIFE

A website developer creates the layout, color scheme, and general design of a website. They create specialized, eye-catching websites for the sports industry. They are also responsible for the site's technical aspects, including its performance (speed) and capacity (traffic). They may work for a company or organization directly. They may also be hired independently. Because every organization is different, web developers work with each client to create an individual design that appeals to customers and fans. Web developers then take their design and create a website. After the site is built, they regularly adjust and add updates to the site. In some cases, web developers also create content for the website. On a project, a website developer might:

- Meet with clients or management to discuss the needs and design of a website
- Create and test applications for a website
- Write code for websites, using programming languages such as HTML or XML
- Work with other team members to determine what information the site will contain
- Work with graphics and other designers to determine the website's layout
- Integrate graphics, audio, and video into the website

- Monitor website traffic

Because every website is different, web developers customize each site for their clients' needs. For example, websites for sporting goods stores need e-commerce applications so that they can sell products online. In contrast, personal websites for athletes might be news focused but include the ability for the athlete to upload home videos to share with fans. Together the web developer and client decide which applications a site need.

Some web developers build an entire website from start to finish. Others specialize in a particular area of web devel-

HTML: THE WEB'S LANGUAGE

Web developers know how to use HTML coding to build websites. "HTML" stands for "HyperText Markup Language." Developed by scientist Tim Berners-Lee in 1990, it is the language used to create web pages that can be displayed in a web browser. HTML uses tags to mark blocks of text on a page. One of the most common HTML tags used is the <strong>, or bold, tag. It is used to mark text that should be bolded. For example, <strong>this is bold text</strong>.

opment. Back-end web developers work on the technical construction of the site. They create the site's framework and make sure that it works as designed. They also add procedures for others to add pages and content in the future. Front-end developers focus on a website's appearance. They design the layout and integrate graphics and other content. Once a website is live, webmasters maintain and update the sites. They monitor the site to make sure everything is working properly and respond to user comments and questions.

PREPARING YOURSELF

There is no standard educational path for a career as a web developer. People who want to work in this field should have strong computer skills and a knowledge of graphic design. Taking courses in web programming languages such as HTML and CSS can help a person prepare for and gain the necessary skills for this career. In addition, classes in programing languages such as JavaScript or SQL and computer programs such as Outlook, Adobe Photoshop, Flash FTP, and Microsoft Project are very beneficial. Classes in graphic design are also helpful, especially if the developer will be working primarily on a website's appearance. Because technology changes rapidly, web developers are expected

A website developer draws an image that will be included in a website's home page. The developer makes sure that the client is happy with the website's appearance.

to keep up-to-date on the latest tools and programming languages.

Some candidates choose to enroll in an associate's degree program in web design, web development, or a similar program in order to gain the skills needed for this career.

Two friends visit a website on a smartphone. Today's website developers consider different-sized screens and devices as they create websites for clients.

In these programs, students learn web basics, along with more challenging classes such as web animation and multimedia design. For very technical positions, such as a back-end web developer, some companies may prefer candidates with a bachelor's degree in computer science, programming, or a related field.

When applying for jobs, web developers are expected to provide a portfolio of web work that they have completed.

In some cases, working as an unpaid intern will help a person gain on-the-job experience while building his or her portfolio.

FUTURE PROSPECTS

As the internet becomes more integrated in daily life and e-commerce expands, the need for websites and web developers is expected to be strong. According to the Bureau of Labor Statistics, employment of web developers is project to grow 27 percent from 2014 to 2024, a rate that is much faster than the average for all occupations. The increase in mobile device use is one factor driving job growth for this career. Web developers will be needed to create websites that work on mobile devices with many different screen sizes. Web developers with experience using multiple programming languages and multimedia tools will have the best opportunities.

FOR MORE INFORMATION

BOOKS

Cooper, Nate, and Kim Gee. *Build Your Own Website: A Comic Guide to HTML, CSS, and WordPress.* San Francisco, CA: No Starch Press, 2014.
This book is a fun, illustrated introduction to the basics of creating a website.

Lopuck, Lisa. *Web Design for Dummies.* 3rd ed. Hoboken, NJ: Wiley, 2012.
This straightforward guide gets readers started on designing, developing, troubleshooting, and launching a website.

Robbins, Jennifer Niederst. *Learning Web Design: A Beginner's Guide to HTML, CSS, JavaScript, and Web Graphics.* 4th ed. Sebastopol, CA: O'Reilly Media, 2012.
This book teaches readers how to use the latest techniques, best practices, and current web standards—including HTML5 and CSS3—to build web pages.

ASSOCIATIONS

International Web Association (IWA)
119 E. Union Street, Suite A
Pasadena, CA 91103

(626) 449-3709
Website: http://iwanet.org
IWA is the industry's recognized leader in providing
educational and certification standards for web
professionals.

Web Professionals
PO Box 584
Washington, IL 61571-0584
(916) 989-2933
Website: https://webprofessionals.org
Web Professionals is a nonprofit professional
association dedicated to the support of individuals
and organizations who create, manage, or market
websites.

WEBSITES

Because of the changing nature of internet links, Rosen
Publishing has developed an online list of websites
related to the subject of this book. This site is updated
regularly. Please use this link to access this list:

http://www.rosenlinks.com/CCWC/sports

GLOSSARY

ANATOMY The branch of science that studies the structure of the human body.

BROADCAST To transmit a program live via television or radio.

CARDIOVASCULAR EXERCISE Any exercise that raises a person's heart rate.

CONDITIONING The process of training to become physically fit.

CUSTOMIZE To modify something to make it specifically for an individual or organization.

DATA ANALYTICS The science of examining raw data in order to draw conclusions about that data.

FREELANCER A person who is self-employed and not committed to a particular employer for a long period.

GRAPHICS An image or a series of images shown on a website.

INCENTIVE Something that motivates a person to do something.

INTERN A student who works, sometimes without pay, to gain experience in a job or trade.

INVENTORY To make a complete list of items or goods in stock.

KINESIOLOGY The scientific study of the human body, also called human kinetics.

NEGOTIATE To deal or bargain with others, such as when preparing a sales contract.

NETWORK To interact with people to exchange information and make contacts, in order to further one's career.

PHYSIOLOGY The branch of biology that studies the normal function of living organisms and their parts.

PORTFOLIO A collection of a person's best artwork that is submitted for review when applying for school or a job.

PROSPECTS People who are believed to be likely to succeed in the future.

STAMINA The ability to keep doing physical exercise over a period of time.

STRENGTH TRAINING A type of exercise that uses resistance to contract the muscles, which builds strength over time.

TRANSMITTERS Equipment that generates and transmits electromagnetic waves to carry radio or television signals.

BIBLIOGRAPHY

Bureau of Labor Statistics. http://www.bls.gov.

Career Research. "Sports Equipment Manager Career."
Retrieved March 30, 2016. http://career.iresearchnet
.com/career-information/sports-equipment-manager
-career.

Clapp, Brian. "Becoming a Sports Equipment Manager."
Work in Sports.com, March 18, 2016. http://www
.workinsports.com/blog/becoming-a-sports
-equipment-manager.

Flood, Alex. "Why you should consider becoming a personal
trainer." List for Life, August 8, 2015. http://www.listforlife.
net/people/consider-becoming
-personal-trainer-766.

Glauber, Bill. "Minor league umpire chases dreams of making
it to the majors." *Journal Sentinel,* June 22, 2013. http://
www.jsonline.com/news/wisconsin/minor-league-
umpire-chases-dreams-of-making-it-to-the-majors-
b9939083z1-212643831.html.

Huff, Pierce. "Behind the scenes of the 'Monday Night Football'
broadcast." *Times-Picayune,* November 29, 2009. http://
www.nola.com/saints/index.ssf/2009/11
/behind_the_scenes_of_the_monda.html.

Kurtz, Annalyn. "Make $30 an hour, no bachelor's degree
required." CNN Money.com, May 25, 2013. http://money
.cnn.com/2013/05/21/news/economy/web-developer-job.

Learn.org. "Sports Photography: Career and Salary Facts."
Retrieved March 5, 2016. http://learn.org/articles/Sports
_Photography_Career_and_Salary_FAQs.html.

Linton, Ian. "Careers in Sports Photography." *Houston Chronicle.*
Retrieved March 5, 2016. http://work.chron
.com/careers-sports-photography-1127.html.

Morissey, Liz. "Darien YMCA Announces New Fitness Directors."
Darien Patch, October 6, 2014. http://patch
.com/connecticut/darien/darien-ymca-announces-new
-fitness-directors-0.

Shapiro, Ben. "Life as a Club Tennis Pro." University of Rochester,
July 22, 2015. http://www.uofrathletics.com
/news/2015/7/22/MTEN_0722150958.aspx.

Storm, Stephanie. "As baseball's trade deadline looms, a day in
the life of a pro scout." *Beacon Journal,* July 23, 2013. http://
www.ohio.com/news/top-stories/as-baseball
-s-trade-deadline-looms-a-day-in-the-life-of-a-pro
-scout-1.415369.

Wong, Wylie. "The NFL Draft Integrates More with Data Analytics."
BizTech.com, May 1, 2015. http://www
.biztechmagazine.com/article/2015/05/nfl-draft
-integrates-more-data-analytics.

Wood, Robert. "Careers in Sport." Topend Sports. Retrieved March
5, 2016. http://www.topendsports
.com/resources/jobs-in-sport.htm.

Work in Sports. http://www.workinsports.com/usrhome.asp

INDEX

ABOUT THE AUTHOR

Carla Mooney is a graduate of the University of Pennsylvania. She writes for young people and is the author of numerous educational books. She is an avid sports fan and enjoys watching football, hockey, baseball, and the Olympics!

PHOTO CREDITS: